A simple CBT practical tools for kids

Interesting, fun exercises and activities to empower your children with strategies to handle anxiety, ADHD and manage feelings

Patricia O. Patrick

GRATITUDE

To all the parents, readers and buyers of this book,

We want to extend our heartfelt gratitude to each and every one of you. Your support, encouragement, and enthusiasm for this book mean the world to us. It is because of your belief in the power of cognitive behavioral therapy (CBT) for children that this book exists, and for that, we are truly grateful.

Parenting is a journey filled with ups and downs, challenges and triumphs. It is our hope that this book serves as a valuable resource and companion on your parenting journey, empowering you to support your child's emotional and mental well-being with confidence and compassion.

We want to thank you for your commitment to your children's growth and development, for your unwavering love and dedication, and for being the superheroes in your children's lives. Your willingness to learn and grow alongside your children is a testament to the power of love, resilience, and the human spirit.

As you begin on this path with us, we want you to know that you are not alone. We are here to support you every step of the way, cheering you on, celebrating your successes, and standing by you through the challenges.

From the bottom of our hearts, thank you for choosing this book, thank you for believing in the transformative power of CBT for children, and thank you for being the amazing parents and caregivers that you are.

With deepest gratitude,
Patricia O. Patrick

7

INTRODUCTION

Welcome to this workbook on teaching cognitive behavioral therapy (CBT) skills to children! As a parent, you play a crucial role in your child's emotional well-being and development. This workbook is designed to equip you with the tools and techniques to help your children steer their thoughts, feelings, and behaviors healthily and positively.

Why Cognitive Behavioral Therapy (CBT) Skills Matter for Children

Childhood is a time of growth, learning, and exploration. It's also a time when children face various challenges that can impact their mental health and well-being. From academic stress to social pressures, children encounter a range of experiences that can trigger negative thoughts and emotions.

This is where cognitive behavioral therapy (CBT) comes in. CBT is a practical and evidence-based approach to therapy that helps individuals understand the connection between their thoughts, feelings, and actions. By teaching children CBT skills, you empower them to recognize and challenge negative thought patterns, manage difficult emotions, and develop healthier coping strategies.

CBT skills are especially valuable for children because they provide practical tools that can be applied to various aspects of their lives. Whether it's dealing with school-related stress, managing anxiety before a big event, or navigating conflicts with friends, CBT equips children with the resilience and confidence to face life's challenges head-on.

Overview of the Workbook

This workbook is divided into several sections, each focusing on different aspects of teaching CBT skills to children. We'll start by exploring the core concepts of CBT and how they apply to children's lives. Then, we'll dig into practical tools and techniques that you can use to teach CBT to your children in a fun and engaging way.

Throughout the workbook, you'll find activities, exercises, and real-life examples to help illustrate key concepts and reinforce learning. Whether you're a parent, caregiver, or educator, this workbook offers valuable insights and resources for supporting children's mental health and well-being.

So let's begin on this journey together and empower our children with the skills they need to thrive emotionally and mentally!

CHAPTER 1

Understanding Cognitive Behavioral Therapy (CBT)

Cognitive Behavioral Therapy (CBT) is like a magic key that unlocks the door to understanding our thoughts, feelings, and actions. It's a bit like having a treasure map for our minds! But what exactly is CBT, and how does it work, especially for children?

What is CBT?

Let's break it down into simple terms. CBT is all about how we think, feel, and behave. Imagine your mind as a big, bustling city. In this city, there are highways of thoughts, bustling streets of feelings, and actions that are like little paths we take. CBT helps us navigate this city better.

How CBT Works for Children

Now, think about being a child. Everything is new and sometimes a bit scary. CBT is like giving kids a special compass to find their way through the ups and downs of growing up. It teaches them to notice their thoughts, understand their feelings, and choose how they want to act.

For example, let's say a child is scared of the dark. With CBT, they can learn that just because they feel scared doesn't mean something bad will happen. They can challenge those scary thoughts and choose to be brave, maybe by imagining a friendly superhero by their side.

Benefits of Teaching CBT to Kids

Teaching CBT to kids is like giving them superpowers for their minds. It helps them feel more confident, resilient, and in control. Here are some of the amazing benefits:

Emotional Resilience: CBT teaches kids to bounce back from tough times. They learn that they have the power to change how they think and feel, even when things seem tough.

Problem-Solving Skills: With CBT, kids become like little detectives, figuring out what's going on in their minds. This helps them solve problems more effectively and make better decisions.

Improved Relationships: When kids understand their thoughts and feelings, they can better understand others too. This leads to stronger friendships and better communication with family members.

Reduced Anxiety and Stress: CBT gives kids the tools to manage their worries and fears. They learn to challenge those anxious thoughts and replace them with more helpful ones, leading to less stress and more peace of mind.

<u>Better Performance:</u> Whether it's in school, sports, or hobbies, CBT helps kids perform at their best. By managing their thoughts and emotions, they can focus better, stay motivated, and achieve their goals.

In essence, teaching CBT to kids is like giving them a roadmap to navigate life's twists and turns with confidence and courage. It's an invaluable gift that equips them for success in both the present and the future.

CHAPTER 2

Getting Started: Setting the Foundation

Setting the foundation for teaching cognitive behavioral therapy (CBT) to children is like building a sturdy house. You need a strong base to support everything else you'll add on later. In this section, we'll traverse how to create a supportive environment and build trust and open communication with your child.

Creating a Supportive Environment

Think of your home as a cozy nest where your child can feel safe, loved, and supported. Creating a supportive environment is like adding warm blankets and soft pillows to make it extra inviting. Here are some ways to do it:

Unconditional Love: Let your child know that your love is always there, no matter what. Show them through hugs, kind words, and quality time together that they are cherished and valued.

Encouragement: Be your child's biggest cheerleader. Celebrate their achievements, no matter how big or small, and encourage them to keep trying, even when things get tough.

Empathy: Put yourself in your child's shoes and try to understand things from their perspective. Let them know that you see and hear them and that their feelings are valid.

Consistency: Children thrive on routines and predictability. Create a consistent and stable environment where they know what to expect and feel secure.

Respect: Treat your child with respect and dignity. Listen to their thoughts and opinions, even if you don't always agree, and involve them in decision-making whenever possible.

By creating a supportive environment at home, you lay the groundwork for your child to feel safe and comfortable exploring their thoughts and feelings.

Building Trust and Open Communication

Trust and open communication are like the glue that holds your relationship with your child together. They create a strong bond that allows you to navigate challenges and share life's joys.

Here's how to build trust and open communication with your child:

Be Present: Put down your phone, turn off the TV, and give your child your full attention when they're talking to you. Show them that they are your top priority.

Listen Actively: Listen not just with your ears, but with your heart. Pay attention to your child's words, tone, and body language, and respond in a way that shows you truly understand.

<u>Validate Feelings:</u> Let your child know that it's okay to feel whatever they're feeling, even if it's not pleasant. Validate their emotions and reassure them that you're there to support them.

<u>Be Honest:</u> Trust is built on honesty. Be truthful with your child, even when it's difficult, and admit when you've made a mistake. Your honesty will strengthen your bond and set a positive example.

<u>Respect Privacy:</u> While open communication is important, so is respecting your child's privacy. Let them know that they can confide in you, but also give them space when they need it.

By building trust and open communication with your child, you create a solid foundation for teaching CBT skills and navigating life's challenges together as a team.

CHAPTER 3

Core Concepts of CBT Explained for Kids

Let's set about on a passage to inspect the core concepts of cognitive behavioral therapy (CBT) in a way that's easy for kids to understand. Think of it like discovering the secrets of a hidden treasure map for your mind!

Thoughts, Feelings, and Actions: The CBT Triangle

Imagine your mind as a big, colorful triangle with three important points: thoughts, feelings, and actions. These three points are connected, just like how a story has a beginning, middle, and end. Here's how they work together:

Thoughts: Thoughts are like little messages that pop into your head. They can be happy, sad, scary, or funny. Sometimes they're true, and sometimes they're not! Our thoughts can affect how we feel and what we do.

Feelings: Feelings are like colorful balloons floating in the sky. They can be big and bright, or small and quiet. Sometimes they make us feel happy and excited, and other times they make us feel sad or scared. Our feelings come from our thoughts and can influence what we do next.

Actions: Actions are like the things we do in response to our thoughts and feelings. They can be big, like climbing a mountain, or small, like hugging someone. Our actions can change how we feel and think, just like how a smile can make us feel happier.

Understanding how thoughts, feelings, and actions are all connected helps us make sense of what's happening in our minds and hearts.

Identifying Thoughts and Feelings

Now, let's put on our detective hats and become thought and feeling detectives! Just like solving a mystery, identifying our thoughts and feelings helps us understand ourselves better. Here's how to do it:

<u>Notice Your Thoughts:</u> Pay attention to the little messages that pop into your head throughout the day. Are they happy thoughts, sad thoughts, or worried thoughts? Write them down in a special notebook or draw them in a picture.

<u>Check Your Feelings:</u> Once you've identified your thoughts, check in with your feelings. How do they make you feel? Are you happy, sad, angry, or scared? Draw a picture of how your feelings look and give them names, like "Happy Harry" or "Worried Wendy."

<u>Connect the Dots:</u> Now, connect the dots between your thoughts and feelings. How do your thoughts make you feel? Do they make you feel happy or sad? And how do your feelings influence what you do next?

Understanding Automatic Negative Thoughts (ANTs)

Imagine your mind as a garden filled with all kinds of flowers and plants. But sometimes, pesky little ants sneak into the garden and start causing trouble. These ants are called Automatic Negative Thoughts (ANTs), and they can make us feel yucky inside.

Here are some common types of ANTs:

Mind Reading: This ANT makes us believe we know what others are thinking, even when we don't. It can make us feel anxious or insecure.

Fortune Telling: This ANT makes us negatively predict the future. It can make us feel worried or scared about things that haven't even happened yet.

All-or-Nothing Thinking: This ANT makes us see things in black and white, with no shades of gray. It can make us feel like we've failed, even when we've done our best.

Labeling: This ANT makes us put negative labels on ourselves or others. It can make us feel bad about ourselves and lower our self-esteem.

Catastrophizing: This ANT makes us blow things out of proportion and imagine the worst-case scenario. It can make us feel overwhelmed and helpless.

But here's the good news: just like we can get rid of pesky ants in the garden, we can squash ANTs in our minds too! By noticing them, challenging them, and replacing them with positive thoughts, we can keep our minds happy and healthy.

CHAPTER 4

Tools and Techniques for Teaching CBT to Children

Now that we've laid the groundwork for understanding cognitive behavioral therapy (CBT), let's go headfirst into some fun and practical tools and techniques for teaching CBT to children. Think of these tools as special gadgets in your mental superhero utility belt, ready to help your child maneuver their thoughts and feelings with confidence and courage!

Mindfulness Exercises

Mindfulness is like taking a mini-vacation for your mind. It helps us focus on the present moment and appreciate the beauty and wonder all around us. Here are some mindfulness exercises you can try with your child:

Breathing Buddies: Find a cozy spot to sit with your child and place a stuffed animal or toy on their belly. Encourage them to take slow, deep breaths, watching their buddy rise and fall with each breath.

Sensory Scavenger Hunt: Take a nature walk with your child and explore the sights, sounds, smells, and textures around you. Encourage them to notice the little details and appreciate the beauty of the world.

Mindful Eating: Choose a favorite snack with your child, like a piece of fruit or a cookie. Before taking a bite, take a moment to observe the color, texture, and smell of the food. Then, savor each bite slowly, paying attention to the taste and sensation in your mouth.

Five-Senses Check-In: Sit with your child and guide them through a five senses check-in. Ask them to notice five things they can see, four things they can touch, three things they can hear, two things they can smell, and one thing they can taste.

These mindfulness exercises help children develop awareness and appreciation for the present moment, which can reduce stress and anxiety and improve overall well-being.

Thought Records and Worksheets

Thought records and worksheets are like detective notebooks for our minds. They help us identify and challenge negative thoughts and replace them with more positive and helpful ones. Here's how to use them with your child:

<u>Identifying Thoughts:</u> Sit down with your child and ask them to write down a recent situation that made them feel sad, worried, or angry. Then, help them identify the thoughts that were going through their mind at the time.

<u>Challenging Thoughts:</u> Once they've identified their thoughts, help your child challenge them by asking questions like, "Is this thought true?" "What evidence do we have to support or refute it?" and "What's another way to look at this situation?"

Replacing Thoughts: Finally, help your child replace their negative thoughts with more positive and helpful ones. Encourage them to come up with realistic and empowering statements that counteract their original thoughts.

These thought records and worksheets help children develop a more balanced and realistic perspective on themselves and the world around them.

Relaxation Techniques

Relaxation techniques are like magic spells that help us banish stress and anxiety and summon feelings of calm and peace. Here are some relaxation techniques you can try with your child:

Deep Breathing: Teach your child the power of deep breathing by taking slow, deep breaths together. Encourage them to imagine filling their belly with air like a balloon and then slowly releasing it.

Progressive Muscle Relaxation: Guide your child through a progressive muscle relaxation exercise, starting with their toes and working their way up to their head. Encourage them to tense and relax each muscle group, releasing any tension they may be holding.

Guided Imagery: Take your child on a guided imagery journey to a peaceful and relaxing place, like a sunny beach or a tranquil forest. Encourage them to use all their senses to fully immerse themselves in the experience.

Mindful Movement: Practice gentle yoga or tai chi movements with your child, focusing on slow and deliberate movements that promote relaxation and mindfulness.

These relaxation techniques help children reduce stress and anxiety, improve concentration and focus, and promote overall feelings of well-being and relaxation.

CHAPTER 5

Applying CBT Skills in Everyday Situations

Now that we've learned about the core concepts and tools of cognitive behavioral therapy (CBT), it's time to put these skills into action in our everyday lives. Think of CBT as your trusty sidekick, ready to help you tackle any challenge that comes your way. In this section, you'll learn about how to apply CBT skills in three common situations: managing anxiety, dealing with frustration and anger, and building resilience.

Managing Anxiety

Anxiety is like a pesky little monster that creeps into our minds and makes us feel scared and worried. But with CBT skills, we can tame that monster and reclaim our sense of calm and control. Below are some tips for managing anxiety:

<u>Recognize Triggers:</u> Pay attention to the things that trigger your anxiety, whether it's a big test at school, a social gathering, or a crowded place. Once you know your triggers, you can better prepare yourself to face them.

<u>Challenge Negative Thoughts:</u> When anxious thoughts start swirling in your mind, challenge them with CBT techniques. Ask yourself questions like, "Is this thought realistic?" "What evidence do I have to support it?" and "What's a more balanced way to think about this?"

<u>Practice Relaxation Techniques:</u> Use relaxation techniques like deep breathing, progressive muscle relaxation, and guided imagery to calm your mind and body. Take slow, deep breaths, tense and relax your muscles, and imagine yourself in a peaceful and soothing place.

Take Action: Instead of avoiding the things that make you anxious, face them head-on and take small, manageable steps to overcome your fears. Start with baby steps and gradually work your way up to bigger challenges.

Practice Self-Care: Take care of yourself physically, mentally, and emotionally. Get plenty of sleep, eat nutritious foods, exercise regularly, and engage in activities that bring you joy and relaxation.

Dealing with Frustration and Anger

Frustration and anger are like fiery dragons that can quickly spiral out of control if left unchecked. But with CBT skills, we can learn to tame these dragons and respond to challenging situations with calm and clarity. Here's how to deal with frustration and anger:

Pause and Take a Breath: When you feel frustration or anger bubbling up inside you, take a moment to pause and take a deep breath. This simple act can help you calm your emotions and think more clearly.

<u>Identify Triggers:</u> Pay attention to the things that trigger your frustration and anger, whether it's a difficult task, a disagreement with a friend, or a change in plans. Once you know your triggers, you can better prepare yourself to respond calmly.

<u>Challenge Negative Thoughts:</u> Just like with anxiety, challenge negative thoughts that fuel your frustration and anger. Ask yourself questions like, "Is this situation as bad as I'm making it out to be?" "What's another way to look at this?" and "What can you do to solve this problem?"

<u>Use Problem-Solving Skills:</u> Instead of reacting impulsively, use problem-solving skills to address the source of your frustration or anger. Break the problem down into smaller steps, brainstorm possible solutions, and choose the best course of action.

<u>Practice Empathy:</u> Put yourself in the other person's shoes and try to understand their perspective. This can help you respond with empathy and compassion, rather than anger and hostility.

Building Resilience

Resilience is like a superpower that helps us bounce back from tough times and emerge stronger than ever. With CBT skills, we can build resilience and weather life's storms with grace and courage. Some ways to build resilience:

Cultivate Optimism: Focus on the positives in life and look for silver linings in difficult situations. Practice gratitude and optimism, even in the face of adversity.

Develop Problem-Solving Skills: Learn to approach challenges with a problem-solving mindset. Break problems down into manageable steps, brainstorm creative solutions, and take action to overcome obstacles.

Build Social Support: Surround yourself with supportive friends and family members who lift you and encourage you to keep going, even when times get tough. Lean on them for guidance, encouragement, and emotional support.

Practice Self-Compassion: Be kind to yourself and treat yourself with the same compassion and understanding that you would offer to a friend in need. Acknowledge your strengths and accomplishments, and forgive yourself for any mistakes or setbacks along the way.

Embrace Change: Life is full of ups and downs, twists and turns. Instead of resisting change, embrace it as an opportunity for growth and self-discovery. Adapt to new challenges with flexibility and resilience, knowing that you have the strength and courage to overcome anything that comes your way.

CHAPTER 6

CBT Activities and Exercises for Kids

Let's get into the world of cognitive behavioral therapy (CBT) activities and exercises for kids! Think of these activities as fun games and adventures that help children explore their thoughts, feelings, and behaviors in a positive and empowering way. In this part of the book, we'll take a look at three exciting CBT activities: role-playing scenarios, creative journaling prompts, and fun mindfulness games.

Role-Playing Scenarios

Role-playing scenarios are like mini-dramas where kids can step into different roles and explore how they would think, feel, and behave in different situations. It's like putting on a costume and becoming a character in your own story! Below is a few role-playing scenarios you can try with your child:

<u>The Brave Knight:</u> Pretend to be a brave knight on a quest to conquer their fears. Encourage your child to face imaginary dragons and monsters (representing their fears and worries) and come up with creative ways to overcome them.

<u>The Wise Wizard:</u> Imagine being a wise wizard with magical powers to change negative thoughts into positive ones. Help your child practice casting spells (using positive affirmations) to banish their worries and fears.

The Friendly Explorer: Take a look at different emotions and how they make us feel. Pretend to be friendly explorers discovering new lands (representing different emotions) and sharing stories about how they make us feel.

The Superhero Team: Assemble a team of superheroes with special powers to tackle challenges together. Each superhero (representing different CBT skills) brings their strengths and abilities to the team, helping each other overcome obstacles and save the day.

Role-playing scenarios are not only fun and engaging, but they also provide valuable opportunities for children to practice problem-solving, empathy, and emotional regulation skills in a safe and supportive environment.

Creative Journaling Prompts

Creative journaling prompts are like magic keys that unlock the door to our innermost thoughts and feelings. They encourage children to express themselves creatively through writing, drawing, and storytelling. Here are some creative journaling prompts you can try with your child:

The Feelings Tree: Draw a tree with branches and leaves. On each leaf, write or draw a different emotion (happy, sad, angry, scared, etc.). Encourage your child to fill in the leaves with their feelings and experiences.

The Storybook Adventure: Write a story together about a character who faces a challenge and learns to overcome it using CBT skills. Encourage your child to think about how the character feels and what they do to solve their problem.

The Gratitude Journal: Start a gratitude journal where your child can write down three things they're grateful for each day. This helps them focus on the positives in their life and cultivate a sense of gratitude and appreciation.

The Dream Diary: Encourage your child to keep a dream diary where they can write down their dreams and explore the thoughts and feelings behind them. This can help them understand their subconscious mind and uncover hidden fears and desires.

Creative journaling prompts provide children with a safe and creative outlet for exploring their thoughts, feelings, and experiences, while also promoting self-reflection, emotional expression, and self-discovery.

Fun Mindfulness Games

Mindfulness games are like playful adventures that help children develop awareness, focus, and relaxation skills. They encourage children to engage their senses and stay present in the moment. See below some fun mindfulness games you can try with your child:

<u>The Five Senses Game:</u> Take turns naming five things you can see, four things you can touch, three things you can hear, two things you can smell, and one thing you can taste. This helps children engage their senses and stay grounded in the present moment.

The Mindful Listening Game: Sit quietly together and listen for different sounds around you, both near and far. Encourage your child to notice the sound of their breath, the rustle of leaves, the chirping of birds, and other sounds in their environment.

The Body Scan Game: Lie down together and take turns scanning your bodies from head to toe, noticing any areas of tension or discomfort. Encourage your child to breathe deeply and relax each part of their body as they go.

The Mindful Eating Game: Choose a favorite snack and eat it slowly and mindfully, paying attention to the taste, texture, and sensation in your mouth. Encourage your child to savor each bite and notice how it makes them feel.

Mindfulness games are not only enjoyable and relaxing, but they also help children develop important skills like focus, attention, and self-awareness, which can improve their overall well-being and quality of life.

CHAPTER 7

Parental Guidance: Supporting Your Child's CBT Journey

As a parent, you play a crucial role in supporting your child or children with cognitive behavioral therapy (CBT). Think of yourself as the captain of a ship, guiding your child through the ups and downs of guiding their thoughts and feelings. In this segment you'll discover strategies for encouraging and reinforcing CBT skills, as well as helming challenges and setbacks along the way.

Strategies for Encouraging and Reinforcing CBT Skills

Encouragement and reinforcement are like sunshine and water for your child's CBT skills, helping them grow and flourish. Some strategies for supporting your child's CBT journey:

Celebrate Progress: Take time to celebrate your child's progress, no matter how small. Whether they successfully challenge a negative thought, manage their anxiety in a new situation, or use a relaxation technique to calm down, praise their efforts and accomplishments.

Provide Positive Feedback: Offer specific and genuine praise for your child's CBT skills. Instead of simply saying, "Good job," try saying something like, "I'm proud of you for using your deep breathing to calm down when you felt anxious. That takes courage and strength!"

Model CBT Skills: Be a role model for your child by practicing CBT skills yourself. Share your own experiences of using mindfulness, thought-challenging, or relaxation techniques to cope with stress and manage your emotions. This shows your child that CBT skills are valuable tools for people of all ages.

<u>**Create a Supportive Environment:**</u> Foster an environment at home that encourages open communication, empathy, and self-expression. Listen to your child without judgment, validate their feelings, and offer support and guidance when needed.

<u>**Set Realistic Expectations:**</u> Be realistic about your child's progress and don't expect perfection. Understand that learning CBT skills takes time and practice and that setbacks are a natural part of the learning process.

By encouraging and reinforcing your child's CBT skills, you provide them with the support and encouragement they need to navigate life's challenges with confidence and resilience.

Navigating Challenges and Setbacks

Just like a ship encountering rough seas, your child's CBT journey may face challenges and setbacks along the way. But with your guidance and support, they can weather the storm and emerge stronger than ever. Here are some strategies for maneuvering challenges and setbacks:

<u>Validate Their Feelings:</u> When your child faces a setback, validate their feelings and let them know that it's okay to feel disappointed, frustrated, or upset. Offer empathy and understanding, and reassure them that you're there to support them no matter what.

<u>Problem-Solve Together:</u> Encourage your child to problem-solve and brainstorm solutions to overcome challenges. Break the problem down into smaller steps, explore different options, and come up with a plan of action together.

<u>Focus on Growth:</u> Shift the focus from the setback itself to the growth and learning that comes from overcoming it. Help your child reframe the situation as an opportunity to learn and grow, rather than a failure or defeat.

<u>Offer Support and Encouragement:</u> Be a source of support and encouragement for your child during challenging times. Offer words of encouragement, hugs, and reassurance that you believe in their ability to overcome obstacles and succeed.

<u>Seek Professional Help if Needed:</u> If your child is struggling with persistent challenges or setbacks, consider seeking support from a mental health professional who specializes in CBT for children. A trained therapist can provide additional guidance and support tailored to your child's unique needs.

By traversing obstacles and setbacks with patience, empathy, and resilience, you help your child build the confidence and skills they need to overcome obstacles and thrive emotionally and mentally.

CHAPTER 8

Case Studies and Real-Life Examples

Imagine sitting around a cozy campfire, sharing stories that warm your heart and ignite your imagination. That's what case studies and real-life examples do in the world of cognitive behavioral therapy (CBT). They paint a vivid picture of how CBT skills can transform lives and inspire hope. This part you'll go down into captivating stories of children applying CBT skills and share success stories from families who have embraced the power of CBT.

Stories of Children Applying CBT Skills

Meet Sarah, a bright and imaginative 10-year-old girl who struggled with anxiety about going to school. Every morning, Sarah would wake up with a knot in her stomach, worrying about what the day would bring. But with the help of CBT skills, Sarah learned to face her fears head-on and reclaim her confidence.

One day, Sarah's CBT therapist introduced her to the "Worry Jar" technique. Together, they decorated a jar with colorful stickers and wrote down Sarah's worries on slips of paper. Every time Sarah worried, she would write it down and place it in the jar. Then, at the end of the day, she and her mom would sit down together and talk about the worries in the jar.

As Sarah continued to use the Worry Jar technique, she noticed that her worries started to feel less overwhelming. She began to see that her worries were just thoughts, not facts and that she had the power to challenge and change them. With each passing day, Sarah's confidence grew stronger, and her anxiety about school began to fade away.

Another inspiring story comes from Daniel, a spirited 8-year-old boy who struggled with anger and frustration when things didn't go his way. Daniel's parents were at their wits' end, unsure of how to help him manage his intense emotions. But with the guidance of a CBT therapist, they discovered a powerful tool for Daniel: the "Anger Meter."

The Anger Meter was a simple chart that Daniel could use to track his anger levels throughout the day. Whenever Daniel felt himself getting angry, he would rate his anger on a scale from 1 to 10 and write down what triggered it. Then, he and his parents would brainstorm healthy ways to calm down and cope with his anger, like taking deep breaths, counting to ten, or talking to a trusted adult.

As Daniel became more aware of his anger and learned to manage it in healthy ways, he felt a sense of empowerment and control. Instead of exploding with anger, he was able to express himself calmly and assertively, improving his relationships with family and friends.

These stories of children applying CBT skills remind us that no matter how big or small the challenge, there is hope and help available. With the right tools and support, children can learn to overcome their struggles and thrive emotionally and mentally.

Success Stories from Families

Now, let's shift our focus to the stories of families who have embraced the power of CBT and witnessed transformative changes in their lives. Meet the Smith family, who struggled with communication and conflict resolution until they discovered CBT techniques for families.

The Smiths were like any other family, with their share of ups and downs. But when disagreements and arguments became a daily occurrence, they knew they needed help. That's when they turned to family therapy and learned CBT skills for improving communication and resolving conflicts.

One of the most valuable tools the Smiths learned was the "I-Message" technique. Instead of blaming and accusing each other during disagreements, they learned to express their feelings and needs using "I" statements. For example, instead of saying, "You always ignore me," they would say, "I feel ignored when you don't listen to me."

As the Smiths practiced using I-Messages and other CBT techniques, they noticed a dramatic improvement in their family dynamics. Communication became more open and honest, conflicts were resolved more peacefully, and bonds grew stronger. They realized that by working together and applying CBT skills, they could create a happier and healthier family environment.

Another heartwarming success story comes from the Johnson family, who struggled with their daughter's bedtime fears and anxieties. Every night, 6-year-old Emily would beg her parents to stay with her until she fell asleep, terrified of monsters under the bed and shadows in the closet.

At their wits' end, the Johnsons sought help from a CBT therapist who specializes in childhood anxiety. Together, they developed a bedtime routine and coping strategies to help Emily overcome her fears. They created a "Bravery Chart" where Emily could earn stickers for facing her fears and staying in her room at night.

As Emily bravely faced her bedtime fears and used her coping strategies, her confidence grew stronger, and her anxieties began to fade away. With each passing night, she became more independent and self-assured, eventually sleeping soundly through the night without any help from her parents.

These success stories from families demonstrate the transformative power of CBT in improving relationships, managing emotions, and fostering resilience. By learning and applying CBT skills together, families can overcome challenges, strengthen bonds, and create a brighter future for themselves and their children.

CHAPTER 9

Frequently Asked Questions (FAQs) About Teaching CBT to Children

Teaching cognitive behavioral therapy (CBT) to children can raise many questions and concerns for parents, caregivers, and educators. In this part of this book, you'll take a look at some of the most frequently asked questions about teaching CBT to children, addressing common concerns and misconceptions along the way. Think of this as your go-to guide for sailing the ins and outs of teaching CBT to children with confidence and clarity.

<u>Q: What exactly is cognitive behavioral therapy (CBT), and how does it work for children?</u>

A: Cognitive behavioral therapy (CBT) is a type of therapy that focuses on the connection between thoughts, feelings, and behaviors. It teaches children to recognize and challenge negative thoughts and replace them with more positive and helpful ones. CBT helps children develop coping skills to manage stress, anxiety, depression, and other emotional challenges, ultimately empowering them to live happier and healthier lives.

<u>Q: Is CBT suitable for all children, or are there specific ages or conditions where it's more effective?</u>

A: While CBT can be beneficial for children of all ages, it may be more effective for older children and adolescents who have the cognitive and emotional maturity to understand and apply the concepts. However, adaptations can be made to make CBT more accessible for younger children, such as using age-appropriate language, visuals, and interactive activities.

Q: How can I introduce CBT to my child in a way that's engaging and understandable?

A: Introducing CBT to your child in a way that's engaging and understandable can be as simple as having open and honest conversations about thoughts, feelings, and behaviors. Use everyday examples and language that your child can relate to, and incorporate fun and interactive activities like games, role-playing, and creative expression.

Q: What if my child doesn't want to participate in CBT or seems resistant to the idea?

A: It's normal for children to feel hesitant or resistant to trying something new, especially if it involves talking about their thoughts and feelings. Be patient and understanding, and try to address any concerns or fears they may have. You can also involve them in the decision-making process and give them choices and autonomy in how they participate in CBT.

Q: Can I teach CBT skills to my child at home, or do I need to seek professional help?

A: While it's possible to teach some CBT skills to your child at home, especially through books, resources, and online courses, it's often beneficial to seek professional help from a trained therapist who specializes in working with children. A therapist can provide personalized guidance, support, and feedback tailored to your child's unique needs and circumstances.

Q: How long does it take for children to see the benefits of CBT, and how can I track progress?

A: The timeline for seeing benefits from CBT can vary depending on the child's age, personality, and the nature of their challenges. Some children may see improvements in a few weeks, while others may take longer. It's essential to track progress by setting specific goals, monitoring changes in thoughts and behaviors, and celebrating milestones along the way.

Addressing Common Concerns and Misconceptions

Now that we've answered some frequently asked questions about teaching CBT to children let's address some common concerns and misconceptions:

Concern: CBT is only for children with diagnosed mental health conditions.

Misconception: While CBT is often used to treat mental health conditions like anxiety, depression, and ADHD, it can also be beneficial for children experiencing everyday challenges like stress, low self-esteem, and difficulty managing emotions.

Concern: CBT is too complicated for children to understand.

Misconception: CBT can be adapted to make it accessible and understandable for children of all ages and developmental levels. By using age-appropriate language, visuals, and interactive activities, children can grasp the concepts of CBT and apply them in their daily lives.

Concern: CBT is just talking about feelings and won't solve anything.

Misconception: While talking about feelings is an essential part of CBT, it's not the only component. CBT teaches children practical skills and strategies for identifying and challenging negative thoughts, managing emotions, and changing behaviors. These skills can have a profound and lasting impact on children's well-being and quality of life.

Concern: CBT is too rigid and doesn't allow for creativity and self-expression.

Misconception: CBT can be flexible and adaptable, allowing for creativity and self-expression. Therapists and educators can incorporate art, storytelling, role-playing, and other creative activities into CBT sessions to engage children and encourage them to express themselves in meaningful ways.

By addressing common concerns and misconceptions about teaching CBT to children, we can create a better understanding of its benefits and potential applications. With patience, empathy, and creativity, parents, caregivers, and educators can help children develop the skills and resilience they need to thrive emotionally and mentally.

CONCLUSION

As we reach the end of this book prospecting cognitive behavioral therapy (CBT) for children, let's take a moment to reflect on the progress and growth we've witnessed along the way. Like a garden bursting with blooms, each child's voyage with CBT is a testament to the power of resilience, determination, and love.

Celebrating Progress and Growth

Throughout this expedition, we've seen children face their fears, challenge their negative thoughts, and develop valuable skills for managing their emotions and behaviors. We've witnessed moments of courage, resilience, and triumph as children embrace their inner strength and navigate life's challenges with grace and confidence.

Let's celebrate the progress and growth of every child who has taken up this journey, no matter how big or small their victories may seem.

From the brave knight who conquers his fears to the friendly explorer who discovered new lands of self-discovery, each step forward is a cause for celebration and joy.

<u>Final Words of Encouragement</u>

As we bid farewell to this passage, let's leave behind a few words of encouragement for all the parents, caregivers, educators, and children who are just starting on their own CBT journey:

To the parents: You are the guiding light that illuminates your child's path. Your love, support, and encouragement are the foundation upon which they build their confidence and resilience. Keep believing in your child's potential and celebrate their growth every step of the way.

To the children: You are brave, strong, and capable of amazing things. Remember that it's okay to feel scared, anxious, or uncertain at times. You have a toolkit full of CBT skills to help you face your fears, challenge your thoughts, and overcome any obstacle that comes your way. Believe in yourself, and never forget how far you've come.

To the caregivers and educators: You play a vital role in shaping the hearts and minds of the next generation. Your dedication, compassion, and guidance empower children to reach their full potential and live their best lives. Keep nurturing their curiosity, creativity, and resilience, and watch them soar to new heights.

Finally, the part of teaching cognitive behavioral therapy to children is not just about overcoming challenges; it's about embracing growth, resilience, and the power of the human spirit. With love, support, and determination, children can learn to overcome life's twists and turns with confidence, courage, and grace. So let's celebrate their progress, encourage their growth, and inspire them to shine brightly as they begin on their unique path of self-discovery and empowerment.

www.ingramcontent.com/pod-product-compliance
Lightning Source LLC
Chambersburg PA
CBHW051700230720
48653CB00007B/2770